Onward Journey

Onward Journey

Seeking the Divine

JOHN BARTRAM REHM

RESOURCE *Publications* · Eugene, Oregon

ONWARD JOURNEY
Seeking the Divine

Resource Publications
An Imprint of Wipf and Stock Publishers
199 W. 8th Ave., Suite 3
Eugene, OR 97401
www.wipfandstock.com

ISBN 13: 978-1-60899-923-1

Manufactured in the U.S.A.

Red Barge, Reflections, 1931, Oil on canvas. The Phillips Collection,
Washington D.C. Copyright: The Estate of Arthur G. Dove, courtesy
of Terry Dintenfass, Inc.
Particular thanks to Toni Dove for her generosity in allowing the use
of the Arthur G. Dove images.

For Diane

Contents

∾ ∾ ∾

Acknowledgments

With DEEPEST gratitude, I wish to recognize the contributions of a number of persons to the creation of this book.

One of the earliest readers of the book was The Rev. Dr. James D. Anderson, author and theologian. The Very Rev. Martha J. Horne, former Dean and President of Virginia Theological Seminary, referred me to Richard Bass, Director of Publishing, The Alban Institute, who recommended that I speak with a renowned editor, Ulrike Guthrie, with whom I have been privileged to work over the last year. She proved to be not only a superb editor, in all respects, but a trusted friend and guide.

That path of progress would never have begun without the strength and caring of my dear friend and Godmother, The Rt. Rev. Jane Holmes Dixon.

Finally, the book would not have come into being without the love and support of my wife, Diane. She believed in me, especially in those times of self-doubt.

John Bartram Rehm
March 27, 2011

List of Images

Arthur G. Dove, *Movement No.1*, c.1911

1

Prologue

INQUIRIES

An explosion?
Yes.

Where?
In the upper room.

How many?
Thirteen.

Seated?
At supper.

Of. . . ?
Bread and wine.

Just bread and wine?
Something else.

What?
Body and blood.

Whose?
His.

Where?
Throughout the room.

The signs?
A shattered table.

And?
Splintered benches.

Where is he now?
Listen.

To what?
The steady rain.

Yes?
And rolling thunder.

When was this?
Yesterday, today, tomorrow.

FLOAT

During the summer months, the three boys often came to the secluded area of the lake front, rocky and beachless. Tan and naked, they gleefully ran across the water to the float they had built and anchored in the middle of the lake. There they leapt off the diving board, played water tag, and sprawled on the weathered boards. After drying in the sun, they sauntered back on the small waves to the shore. One day, their physics teacher, dressed in a dark suit, unexpectedly came upon them. He patiently explained the behavior appropriate to the medium. In particular, he admonished them that one walks on land and swims in water. Like levitation, aquambulation is unseemly and to be discouraged. Therefore, in the summers that followed, the three boys dutifully swam to the float and back, barely recalling the joy of racing on the sparkling buoyant surface of the lake.

MY SPIRITUAL JOURNEY

Until the summer of 1979 and until my middle age I upheld my parents' disdain for all things religious. My father had found the Lutheran Church sterile and irrelevant, as had my mother the Episcopalian Church. I do not recall seeing a copy of the Bible in our home. Indeed, the word "God" was used only as an expletive in our household. Small wonder that the interior of a church remained a mystery to me.

In devising a personal code of conduct, I could count upon no one in my intellectual environment. I therefore fell back upon myself and, not surprisingly, fashioned a code based upon the individual pitted against a hostile and absurd universe. It was called existentialism, which was very much in vogue after World War II.

Existentialism assumes that the only reality is what our senses perceive within the brief span of our mortal being. It preaches a grim self-reliance and affords little refuge from the horrors of contemporary life.

In the spring of 1979, I adopted the practice of dropping in at local churches at different hours. I would engage in an informal kind of meditation, with no particular substance or direction. Something was at work within me, although my conscious being was puzzled.

Then came June 23, 1979, a sparkling summer morning in Manhattan. I was walking up Fifth Avenue to have lunch with my mother near the Metropolitan Museum of Art. I came to 52nd Street and found myself spontaneously entering St. Thomas Church. I sat down in one of the pews. There were only a few other people in the church.

The following events then took place in an extraordinarily rapid succession. I became aware of a Baroque air being rehearsed by an organist. The first line of Gerard Manley Hopkins' poem "The Windhover: To Christ our Lord" leaped to mind: "I caught this morning morning's minion, kingdom of daylight's dauphin, dapple-dawn-drawn Falcon. . . . " It was then blindingly clear that Christ had caught me, and His presence flooded every part of my being. He leveled the massive stone wall I had amassed against Him over the years. For a timeless duration, I sobbed uncontrollably in a paroxysm of joy. I left the church a new man and Christ's own.

Later that year I was baptized into the Episcopal church. Two of my dearest friends served as godfather and godmother. Over the next ten years, I attended Wesley Theological Seminary in Washington D.C. and obtained the degree of Master of Theological Studies. In those studies I was particularly drawn to the Christian mystics, such as Teresa of Avila and St. John of the Cross. Their teachings lie at the heart of this book.

In my continuing spiritual journey I have become increasingly convinced of two truths: first, that each individual has the capacity to be touched by the Divine and thereby to be made whole; second, that the combination of reason and materialism are literally destroying the world and its creatures, human and otherwise. This little book is implicitly a plea for the reinstitution of love and peace—as opposed to hatred and war—as the animating principles of life. Perhaps you will find your own search for the Divine reflected in it.

FLY

From its superior vantage, the polyoptic fly looked up at its grotesque foe. The fly discerned a suspended head, joined to a shoulder, from which projected a flailing arm. The foe shuffled its cumbersome feet across the ceiling, vainly attempting to follow the fly's path. The nimble fly, secure on its ground, derided its foe's unfortunate position. To try to swat a lively fly upside down seemed a double disadvantage. It caused the fly to wonder why the world's creatures should be divided between those who stand upright and those who hang head down. Should not the heavy weight of its foe cause it to plummet from the ceiling and strike its head—perhaps fatally—on the fly's firm ground? If their spatial positions were reversed, would this foe have the upper—or lower—hand? Not given to speculations on relativism, the fly was content to continue to evade the ineffectual swatting of its disoriented foe.

DOOR

The young woman came up the long walk to the weathered house atop the hill. The house was shadowed in the late afternoon, and its interior dark. She seized the worn knob of the front door, turned it firmly, and pushed to open it, as she had done so often in the past. To her surprise, the door resisted. She turned the knob harder and pressed the jamb with her other hand. The door stubbornly refused to open. She stepped back, as though to assure herself that this was the right house. Shaking her head, she walked around the house, looking at the lawn, the withered flowers, the gray clapboard siding. Returning to the door, she turned the knob and gently, hesitantly pushed. Whereupon the door swung open to the warm kitchen.

BLADES OF GRASS

He had been in prison for a number of months, and he still had received no explanation for his incarceration. His arrest, trial, and conviction were a confused recollection, but for the dominant sense of their inexorability. From the time of his involuntary trip to the precinct station, dressed only in his pajamas, he felt embroiled in a sinister process he could not affect, much less control. It was tacitly understood that he was to answer all of their questions but expect no response to his own.

In prison, they gave him few dispensations, but one came to afford vital pleasure. Once a day, he was allowed to walk about a walled courtyard. There grew patches of grass, together with random flowers and several fruit trees. These otherwise humble signs of life became precious amidst the blocks of concrete and steel.

Over time, he realized that he was allowed to stroll in a steadily decreasing part of the courtyard. He first thought that this constituted punishment for his continuing efforts to ascertain why he was in prison at all. Even after he abandoned such efforts, however, the area of dispensation dwindled even more. If he strayed outside the established bounds, they beat him. He had to be content with only patches of grass and a flower or two.

Finally, they restricted him to a narrow pavement of the courtyard. In a crack of the pavement grew a few blades of grass. They absorbed all of his attention when he was let out from his cell. His concentration was so intense that he took back in his mind a vivid image of their details. That image required, however, daily refreshment by immediate contact with the blades of grass. He sometimes wondered how he would hold onto his sanity if they should disappear.

A drought came to afflict the region where the prison was located. During his confined stroll each day, he felt the withering heat and saw the green turn to brown. The condition of his blades of grass grew particularly alarming. He was not allowed to water them, and he saw them begin to die from the drought. Their imminent death seemed to presage his own.

After the blades of grass had shriveled and crumbled to the pavement, he fell into a deep depression and would not go out into the courtyard. His vitality, long sustained by the green plants of the courtyard, had dried up with them. His hours became a series of mechanical actions without purpose or joy. Vacant days and restless nights merged into an absurd continuum.

One day, he was stirred to go outdoors, although the drought had not abated. He mindlessly went to the pavement he had known so well and was astonished to see his blades of grass. They stood fresh and green, still covered with morning dew. When he reached out to touch them, however, he felt nothing. Yet their presence was too potent to deny. Suddenly he understood. It mattered not whether the blades of grass were there, so long as he and they were together here. From that time on, their union was indestructible, and joy flowed back into his life.

Arthur G. Dove, *Red Sun,* 1935

2

Tales of Jesus

Given the intimacy of my conversion to Christ, in my studies I pursued a curriculum that was Christocentric. This enabled me to put my conversion in an historical, as well as spiritual, context. Each of the following couplets invokes an event during or shortly after Jesus' life based upon the accounts in the New Testament. I hope that these little poems will prove to be inspiring.

LOGOS

From the start there was the word
Lives of all to undergird.

BABE

Swaddled safe from hate and spite,
Vaulting dark he soars to light.

MARY

Mary sings a lullaby,
Wondering will he live or die.

JOSEPH

Joseph father in name only
Bore his duty grim and lonely.

JOHN THE BAPTIST

John mid-Jordan washed the one
Heralded to be the son.

TEMPTATION

By the devil tempted thrice,
His soul he would not sacrifice.

PETER

Peter thrice the hapless cheater
Flees his master all the fleeter.

WATER-WALKING

Peter, faithful, water-walks;
Tripped by doubt, his spirit balks.

WEDDING WINE

Turned he water into wine,
Wedding human and divine.

BREAD AND FISH

Multiply, he orders loud,
the fish and bread for hungry crowd.

JESUS' MISSION

In our souls with love he deals
And loving teaches, preaches, heals.

JAMES

James for fish was wont to trawl,
Then our souls he learned to haul.

NARD

She poured the nard upon his head,
Looking toward his death ahead.

MONEY CHANGERS

Whipping money changers out,
Cleansed he temple of all doubt.

FIG TREE

Angered by the fig-less tree,
He commanded: Cease to be.

ZACCHAEUS

Little man, to see him clear
He climbed the sycamore so dear.

TRANSFIGURATION

On mount, his face shone like sun's flame,
And he was called by holy name.

GARDEN OF GETHSEMANE

Here with sleeping friends he prayed,
By coming suffering dismayed.

PALM SUNDAY

He storms Jerusalem on colt,
Brief king of a benign revolt.

JUDAS

For betrayer's kiss accursed,
Judas suffered bowels to burst.

LAST SUPPER

Supper last in upper room
Sets in motion cosmic boom.

JOHN

John, the favorite, head on chest,
Witnessed revelation blest.

SOLDIERS

Casting knuckles for his clothes,
Greedy soldiers come to blows.

MOB

Death the frenzied mob demands,
And spikes to cross his feet and hands.

SIMON

Simon forced to bear the cross,
Cried the depth of humans' loss.

GOLGOTHA

On to Golgotha, skull's place,
Where he yields to death's embrace.

EMPTY TOMB

Mary Magdalene in gloom,
First revealed the empty tomb.

EASTER SUNDAY

From that Sunday, as he swore,
Cruel death shall be no more.

EMMAUS

At the table breaking bread,
The stranger Lord became instead.

Arthur G. Dove, *Thunderstorm*, 1917–20

3

Ways of Christ

Since my conversion, I have experienced emanations from Christ. I call these experiences "Chrisms." Though not of oil, I nonetheless consider them anointings.

Chrisms are by definition fragmentary, unpredictable, and powerful. They affirm the constant presence of the Divine in our midst. The following poems suggest the rich variety of Chrisms.

THE STRANGER

Day and night I darkly wrestle
With spectral stranger powerful.
Trunks collide, limbs strain and grapple
In naked combat—body stripped,
Soul exposed to bone and sinew.
Immerged in lustral dust and sweat,
Clash we furiously and clamor.
Yields no end or prize our conflict
But his apocalyptic pledge:
Whether and how much you know me,
My passion for you will perdure.

CONVERGENCE

I see him walking ever towards,
His hands and feet yet scarred,
Until we should perchance converge
Where time and space relent,
And pass not by but in and through
Each other, casting back
Upon one's self thus magnified.

BUFFETINGS

Christ knocks and buffets me about,
Jars mind, and senses overturns,
That I might see the fresh afresh
Beyond the sight that smarts and burns.

Relentlessly he shakes my frame
And sets me on the shifting sand,
Unsteady vagrant towards the sill
Where soul may take its holy stand.

At last he leaves me dumb and blind,
In abject nescience of the known,
Until the naught at nadir bursts
Into the substance of his own.

ANCIENT WAYS

In lustrous spray
Fey naiads play.

Lettered yet illiterate
We prize ephemeral words,
Scorning immemorial runes.

Through laurel grove
Shy dryads rove.

Culture courts its vanity
By weight and height of tomes,
Spurning anagogic glyphs.

On bacchic ground
Maenads abound.

Now the times demand that we
Derange the alphabet:
Finally, omega first.

FOLLY

I give the beggarman some coins;
My little gift he may deem wise.
If so, I see Christ's wisdom clear.

But I can hear the cynic claim:
He simply takes you for a fool.
Christ's folly then I hold more dear.

ALTERNATIVES

If Christ does live,
We cease death to misgive
And draw strength to forgive.
If Christ does die,
We live a paltry lie
And end in anguished cry.
If Christ plays neither role,
Treat faith a stubborn goal
Enlivening the soul.

TEARS

I cannot read Cavafy through
The tears that flow this morning:
Tears to celebrate his presence
That comes upon me with a rush
And calls and holds and knows me
His beloved.

EPIPHANY

Abruptly:
    Upon the sidewalk
    In full morning sun,
A fierce dense swarm of ants.

Forcibly:
    Their burnt sienna
    Silhouette creates
An isomorphic fish.

Arthur G. Dove, *Rose and Locust Stump*, 1943

FALL

In morning sadness
Through the wasting park.

Surprised by blooms of
New chrysanthemums:

Ex golden plosions
    of his joy.

TREE

Do we so spurn him in our midst
That we must climb a sycamore
To glimpse his ardent visage from above?

Or must he mount that bitter tree
And stoop to gather us below
Before we grasp the terror of his love?

LEAF

The leaf unseen is better seen
By eyes closed gently to the air
(Not clenched against the shifting green)
And open to the leaf not there.

How can the leaf be more than frail
If we so cling to sight purblind?
Like dervishes we spin and flail
Through endless closets of the mind.

To know the leaf that seems unknown
We start before the branch and tree
And seize the leaf yet to be grown
In unanticipated glee.

LAUGHTER

I meet a stranger on the way;
His conversation strikes me odd.
For he has chosen not to say
But laugh his sense of man and God.

He nods intently as I speak
And shares the lameness of my thought.
His words in turn are spare, oblique;
With laughing his response is fraught.

We bid each other brisk goodbye;
I doubt to meet again his worth.
Afar his laughter claims the sky,
And somber earth bursts into mirth.

SWING

At dusk, the young man took his son to the swing in the wooded park. He set the boy on the seat and put the small hand firmly about each rope. With a delicious mixture of glee and fear, the boy soared to greater and greater heights. It almost seemed he would accomplish a complete revolution, as he heard older boys had done. Coming back to rest, another child took the seat and asked to be pushed up into the evening sky. Thereafter, a series of children emerged from the woods, each expecting to be swung high above the ground. At the zenith of the swing, each child disappeared into the darkening sky, only to be followed by another insistent upon the same aerial experience. The young man lost count of the children he launched into the unknown realm. As he walked home with his son, tired from his exertion, the woods resounded with peals of childish joy.

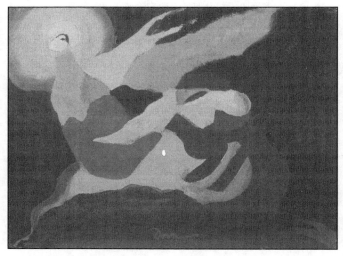

Arthur G. Dove, *The Moon Was Laughing at Me,* 1937

4

Martyred Saints

As a class, the Christian saints epitomize the intensity of the bond that can be experienced with Christ. As martyrs to Christ, the saints experience both physical and spiritual torture. The following poems attempt to communicate that torture by deliberately mangling the traditional sentence structure.

SAINT STEPHEN

Lapidary speech: "Now Christ is all;
By law no longer live—but love."
Sullen rabble screams of blasphemy
Throw back against their God above.

Lithic force of words: "Uncircumcised
In heart, you choked Messiah's breath."
Mob infuriated cobbles pick
And hurl at him to battered death.

Stony silence breaks: "Do not, my Lord,
Against them hold this sin." He sleeps.
Witnesses at feet of Saul lay down
Their garments and depart. Who weeps?

SAINT PERPETUA

Of ardor catechumen ripe,
Her conversion to the king
Despised by Rome constrained arrest,
End barbaric in blood's ring.

With child imprisoned long and friends,
Knowing sport of her they'd make,
Herself male warrior stripped she saw
Skull of devil tread and break.

As though to heaven journeying,
On the day she would contest
High hymn she sang of praise and spurned
Ceres' dress on her they pressed.

In ecstasy, mad heifer's charge
Felt she not nor painful gore.
Exchanging kiss of final peace,
Stilled she rabble's lust and roar.

In body faint but spirit clear,
Gladiator faced she calm
And guided his held knife to throat,
Hazarding death's vital balm.

SAINT IRENE

Homeland low from she ascends
High seclusion to montane,
Setting on her Lord's way forth
Souls to ease by prayer in pain.

Under Diocletian brought
Magistrate before, in heat
Of conviction she adjures
Sacrificial food to eat.

Obdurate, blaspheming, too,
Sanctity of pagan rite,
Naked is for treason sent
Soldiers' brothel to excite.

There no man accost her dares,
And each day soul, body thrive
On one loaf his flesh of bread
Till her fiery death alive.

SAINT BARBARA

Entowered from lascivious eyes
For chastity by father's list,
Illicit union in his ken
She made who rose with Lord from dust.

To dwell she chose in house of bath,
Of soul's ablution anchorite,
And windows two increased by one
To capture Trinitarian light.

By her perversion gross enraged,
He near committed filicide
And her to judge relented who
But death saw fit profane for pride.

Dispatched her father was by bolt
Of lightning from aphotic cloud.
At blow of executioner,
Bedazzled she to shed earth's shroud.

SAINT EUSTACE

Born Placidas, eagle's son,
Loyal soldier he became
General to Trajan sworn.

Met he stag with crucifix
Bright between its antlers and
New his Lord embraced, reborn.

Eagle falls to demigods;
Stag the way enlightened trods.

Taking name of lamb, he bore
Loss of fortune, child, wife,
Till restored command to full.

Scorning pagan sacrifice,
He and gentle family
Roasted were in brazen bull.

Eagle, bull, his puissant foe,
Stag and lamb now overthrow.

SAINT URSULA

Of Christian daughter king,
Her troth she gave in tears
To wed prince pagan, once
Elapsed three virgin years.

This interval of grace
She with companions sailed
Ten ships resplendent and
God's oceans, rivers hailed.

Instead of wife to chief
Of Huns, she chose Christ's bride:
Her Hunnish death would pass
But sacral wedlock bide.

FIVE SAINTS FROM PERSIA

From Persia far five masons to
Imperial city came with tools
To build and skills to carve in stone:
For ruler, servants and Christ, fools.

That stone might manifest its soul,
They shaped of finest hue and feel
Forms wondrous, but to carve refused
Asclepius, believed to heal.

Nor could to pantheon they pray
Or bestial sacrifice attest.
Imprisoned and from drowning dead,
By flowing water they are blessed.

SAINT GEORGE

Lumbered land through dragon,
To kill exhaling fumes and maim.
Lest next victim bride be,
He lanced and girdled beast as tame.

Lucid rose his vision:
Not man but Christ true dragon's foe.
For his Lord and faithful,
He slew fell beast and rid its woe.

Brutish Roman senate
Refined sheer terror to enmesh
Christian cells suspected
Of orgies foul and eating flesh.

Emperor draconic
Him death begrudged as tortures ceased.
Still endures the battle
Between Christ's seeker and his beast.

SAINT SEBASTIAN

Why midair deflects not Christ,
Your savior, arrows' hail
Naked from your body bound,
And you with tears impale?

Victor Diocletian seems
As bristles flesh with bane,
Feet about pools streaming blood,
And yields oblivion pain.

Beaten end cloacal to,
Disgraced praetorian guard,
New now captaincy assume
In saintly corps and scarred.

SAINT AGATHA

Wealth obnoxious sickened by,
Innocence of flesh and soul
Vowed she ever to her Lord—
Gift of light, no darksome toll.

Consul, called Quintinian,
Bound by Rome's malign decree,
Plotted she be foul seduced—
Paradigm of perfidy.

Cast her consul into whores;
Yet her vow she took not back.
First by fire she tortured was,
Then tormented on the rack.

Mutilated breasts were healed
Sighting Peter by the sea.
Death the prisoned body loosed
Soul to join forever free.

SKIP STONE

His father taught him, but he still cannot plumb its fascination. It combines two primal elements—stone and water. It involves motion created by human energy. It serves an ever-receding goal. He is tempted to call it a fugitive act.

Along the water's edge, he must first find the right stone. Its heft should resist the breeze. The first finger and thumb should hold it comfortably. One side should be flat and smooth. Such a stone is worth the quest.

A placid lake provides the best water surface, both to support and witness the stone's trajectory. If the sun plays too brightly on the water, the stone will be lost. An overcast sky on a summer afternoon provides the best setting. Now, stone, water, and sky await him, the human participant.

He throws a few stones into the words to warm up. His arm sweeps sidearm like the blade of a scythe. His wrist snaps smartly as he releases the stone. His eyes watch it strike a tree trunk with a solid, green knock.

Turning to the lake, he is now ready. A smooth black stone rests in his hand, still wet. With a slight running motion, he cocks his arm and then releases the stone. About ten feet from the shore, it makes its first encounter with the water. It then proceeds to skip four more times. At the last strike, it sinks with a plop, releasing a series of expanding concentric circles.

A fiver, he says to himself—not too bad. Over the next half hour, he finds, and throws, a number of stones. His best throw causes the stone to skip nine times. For a second, he thinks it will skip long enough to traverse the lake. He wonders if that is really possible.

Before returning home, he decides to skip one more stone. He discovers a beauty, lying in the shallows. Exercising more grace than strength, he flings it out over the water. In rapid succession, he sees it skip seven, then eight, even nine times. Just then, he turns his head towards the woods and begins to walk away from the beach. He hears the stone continue to skip across the lake at even intervals. With a deep confidence, he knows that his last stone has crossed the lake and now lies on the far beach, still beating.

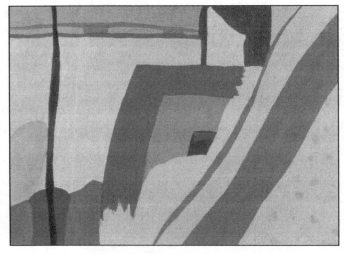

Arthur G. Dove, *Sand Barge,* 1930

5

Lyric Interlude

The following poems celebrate the primacy of the psyche and the subordination of the mind. Accordingly, they elaborate such themes as joy, play, and creativity.

WHITE BLOOMS

Forerain but three
White blooms on stone.

Now seven see:
What souls windthrown?

SHARDS

Whine gnats' why's and sting,
Even prick soul's covering.

What's of bats in flight
Slice across the sacred night.

Thickly whir moths' where's,
Smothering the wisps of prayers.

Who's of hooting owls
Chill young smiles to elders' scowls.

THREE ATTITUDES

I often think,
As years amount,
Two attitudes
Are all that count.

To laugh first at
And then with life,
As humor lifts
the heft of strife.

To weep and all
The world to rue,
And thus bestir
Compassion new.

And yet a third
I would employ;
Tears, laughs combine,
Distilling joy.

AFTRAIN

Like lucent bells from eaves
And ringing faintly leaves
Descend in muted tones
Towards never-reaching stones,
As though back gave to sky
A gift not earth sought by.

RUE

Furled heads of lettuce break apart.
Stout ribs of celery snap in two.
Slim shoots of soul fret, fray, and smart:
Elicits which the deepest rue?

PLAY

Gird the sun and twirl each moon.
Cradle teeming galaxies.
Crescent universe festoon.

In such folly power find
Strength to play outrageously,
Overthrowing rules of mind.

Playfulness may childish seem:
Know you, sage, how better to
Catch the numen's fitful gleam?

PEBBLE

Bright I slipping pebble drop:
Clear down shimmies water far,
On now stream dark bottom rests,
Reach of arm beyond and hand.

From touch far yet to mind close,
Eddies jostled rapid by,
Pebble glows the luminous—
Brighter after-image still.

Longing from would raise the deep
Quick to brightness pebble clear,
Till in hand confirms the sun
Newly treasure's presence found.

UNITIES

In deep embrace
Two shadows strain,

One weeps for joy,
One weeps for pain.

Their lots and tears
So unlike seem,

Each situate
At one extreme.

In truth, their tears
From one source well:

Life's primal need
Change to impel.

And shadows both
In deep embrace

Shape one new life
To take their place.

IMPERATIVES

Be soft, my soul
Consist of gentleness

      Refreshing flow
      Through apertures

Be still, my soul
Desist from word and act

      Of quietude
      Far echoings

Be sound, my soul
Persist to wholeness hale

      From drops of rain
      Integrity

JOURNEYS

In orchard apple blossoms swarm
School of salmon upstream thrash

Remote prey falcon scans
Turtle clambers through burst foam

Leaved and shed tall maple stands
In water deep each ripple dies

Arrivals and departures join
Rampant roads bind near and far

REMBRANDT

Still city's spires in sight,
On curve of river banked,
He strikes to paper pen,
Now child of morning's light.

Of black emerging lines
Arrests on white the scene
Refracted through his eyes
To yield its inmost signs.

With rapid strokes amassed
He riverscapes details
Until foreground confronts
Anticipation vast.

Pen laid, he rests to pond,
Sets mindless eyes adrift,
And draws one boldly line:
Revealing seen's beyond.

LEAF

The leaf unseen is better seen
By eyes closed gently to the air
(Not clenched against the shifting green)
And open to the leaf not there.

How can the leaf be more than frail
If we so cling to sight purblind?
Like dervishes we spin and flail
Through endless closets of the mind.

To know the leaf that seems unknown
We start before the branch and tree
And seize the leaf yet to be grown
In unanticipated glee.

Arthur G. Dove, *Waterfall*, 1925

6

Time and Death

MELANCHOLY

From toil wan and sere,
I satiated my thirst
At well of sadness sweet.

Its waters mind traduce
To life's reflection in
A gray and wistful glass.

Too quickly turns the sweet
To bitter and fulfills
The soul with bile so black.

Dejected fugitive,
I shield myself from light
With head held in my hands.

ROPE OF TIME

The rope of time is long
Yet thin and slippery to
A thousand aching fists
Obsessed with holding on.

The rope of time is frayed
And severs at the touch;
The dangling fall away
Emitting doleful cries.

The rope of time is cruel,
The strangler of our dreams,
Until we throw it off
To stand on timeless ground.

YEARS

How should you count the years?
> Peas fall into the bowl
> Pearls flow from broken strand
> Plums fill upon the branch

Why count them out at all?
> Dried peas will last a while
> Lost pearls may yet be found
> Plum jam makes winter fare

The years are yours to shape:
> Taste now next summer's peas
> Show off the antique pearls
> Pluck every fallen plum

HOPE

Can it be
Too much to hope?
Its account
Is ever full.

Can hope's weight
Be set by rope?
It responds
To gentlest pull.

Of what much
Can exceed hope?
Substance known
To none on earth.

With its sur-
Feit could we cope?
Death for us
To taste its dearth.

CHRONOS

Not as a drowning flood
But trickle time construe.

To time a tidal sweep
We heedlessly confer,

Embittered captives of
What will be, is, and was.

Confess the lunacy
And disempower time.

Contrivance let it be,
A bare pragmatic tool;

In truth, irrelevant
To authenticity.

The real knows naught of time;
Its now is timelessness.

Eternity is found
Precisely where you stand.

DAY

Spill, ah, do not spill the day;
Cup it precious in your palm;

Sweet clear water to allay
Pilgrim's thirst for plunging calm.

DEATH'S WAYS AND MEANS

What transient ways, Death, do you choose?

Spitting cobra's venom
Huge paws of grizzly bear
Panther's deep incisors
Twin pricks of vampire bat
Python's slow constriction
Fierce jaws of soldier ants
Great white shark's predation
Relentless gnaw of rats

What lasting means, Death, heal your bruise?

Luna moth's pulsations
Cavorting vixen's kits
Sperm whale's depthless mating
Ascent of skyward swift
Gray wolf's lope and leaping
Quick thrum of hummingbird
Dolphin's arcing plunges
Sweet industry of bees

Arthur G. Dove, *Flight*, 1943

FLOW

If yester I should die
And but the morrow live,
Would time itself belie
Or stay the fugitive?

If I should live with death,
As a companion dear,
Would mortal be my breath
Or cheat the barren bier?

Blink not at death or life,
The two but seconds span.
With all creation rife,
They flow whence they began.

FALL

In morning sadness
Through the wasting park.

Surprised by blooms of
New chrysanthemums:

Ex golden plosions
          of his joy.

Arthur G. Dove, *Indian One*, 1943

7

Humanity and the Divine

The Divine is, by definition, infinite in all respects. It is therefore beyond the reach of the mind, which perceives reality in ever-smaller finitudes. The following poems and fables try to intimate, however faintly, the presence of the divine in our midst. In particular, they affirm its manifestation in the most humble of circumstances.

SECTIONS

Anatomist proceeds
By sections intricate,
Dissecting whole to parts
And segments into bits.

His learning fittingly
Reposes in great tomes,
Which first were sections of
Papyrus deftly sliced.

Dismemberment, as well,
Engages atomist,
Although his name asserts
The irreducible.

His sections atom split
—No longer primal stuff—
And set loose particles
To roam now-shredded space.

Whatever cutting edge
Analysis performs
Obscures the larger whole,
Blunts play of synthesis.

If mind must ever cleave,
May spirit bind and join,
Lest life but fragments be
And want integrity.

APPLE

Sitting down to the table, the man carefully set the apple upon the white plate. With a pearl-handled fruit knife, he began cutting the apple into sections. From each section he removed the smooth, brown pips. He arranged the pips in a circle around the sections of apple. Leaning back from his task, he smiled and clapped his hands. As though affected by the sound, the pips rose from the plate. With a deft sweep of his hand, he caught them jostling each other in his fist. Upon their release, the pips returned to the sections, the sections joined together, and the apple rested whole again upon the white plate. The man got up from the table, walked to the window, and looked upon the leaves gathering on the ground in the apple orchard.

CORRUPTION

Our self-opposing selves
We pit opposing others,
Thus monstrously corrupt
To hate love-haunted brothers.

POOL

Azaleas brandish at his feet;
The crowd resounds the fool.
I barely catch his voice entreat
    To sound Siloam's pool.

SEEING

The numinous struck William Blake, the boy;
His mind's grid captured angels in a tree.

Red raspberries hard crushed through mesh of sieve
Yield scarlet fractions of their thaumaturgy.

Teresa's flowing inward sight was jammed
By cant in trinitarian pigeonholes.

The wine press renders iridescent grapes
A heavy mess of purple pulp and seeds.

To Francis was revealed pellucid grace,
To reason's scheme, a seraph of six wings.

The delicate profusion of pear shoots
Is hammered on a rigid espalier.

NOTHING

Nothing plays the charlatan;
Its nature seems exclusive.
If to something nothing's foe,
We risk becoming ciphers.

Yet may nothing succor give
To our condition thingless,
Stripping us to vital selves,
The is or not transcended.

Janus-faced this mountebank,
Who, by denying nothing,
Never something substitutes,

SURGERY

If faithful to your principles,
Theologian, scalpel wield
Upon ecclesiastic flesh.
Puncture sacerdotal boils,
Resect obstructive liturgy,
Sever hierarchic fat,
Dissect and credal fractures bind.
Radical your surgery,
If church, proud and parochial, can
First to pilgrims minister,
Exalt their ceaseless, endless quest,
Bare its own satanic deeds,
Embolden laity to take
Ultimately churchless ways.

STONES

The man worked all day repairing the wall of field stones. His hands were rough from their surfaces, and his blue shirt was stained with sweat under the hot June sun. Some of the stones were easily retrieved from the side of the broken wall. By late morning he had entered the rhythm of his labor, stooping, rising, quickly discerning the best seat for each stone, and setting it in its proper place in the wall. He used the larger, flatter stones to cap the wall as he moved through sunlight and shade down its length. Without uttering a single word all day, he continued his labor, pleased with the symmetry of construction. The stones found their place and yet retained their individuality. In late afternoon, he set the final capping stone. As he crossed the meadow, he looked back to admire his work and was startled by the stones' sweet din.

LEONARDO DA VINCI

Scalpel-like, in blood or ink,
His pen dissects the rigid corpse
To display its cords and bones
As moving parts of one machine.

Ceaseless curiosity
Impels the anatomic line
Hanging on the human frame
The spars and rigging of a mast.

Do his analytic eyes
Perceive abyss beyond machine?
Are the ever-meshing parts
Brief signs of what may be beyond?

AT THE ATSUTA SHRINE—NAGOYA

We construe our gods.
Will we ever allow God
To create our lives?

The Shinto priest's chant,
Our shoes striking the gravel:
Which the louder prayer?

Through each gate towards the
Shrine, do I move more into
Or out of myself?

Cold, cleansing water,
Chill, smarting wind: why should they
Warm the spirit so?

Written prayers flutter
In the wind: When will we speak
So God can hear us?

Why do we hurry
Through the cypress archway and
Not rest thereunder?

Fog descends upon
The Shinto shrine: can you see
It more clearly now?

FAIRY RING

At twilight during the summer, the man and his son go out onto the mown field, carrying a bucket of white balls. Each takes a position at his end of the field. Standing a hundred feet or so apart, they begin to throw a white ball back and forth. In the exchange, the ball traces a long and lofty arc against the sky. They laugh to see who can throw it higher than the other and still keep it within the catcher's range.

As the sky darkens, it becomes increasingly hard to detect the flight of the white ball. The thrower calls out to the dimming catcher that he is releasing the ball. After several seconds, the catcher responds that he has caught the ball or lost it in the deepening shadows. Once thrown, the ball hovers ghost-like and then disappears from view, unless spied at the last moment of descent. Soon the supply of white balls is depleted, and the father and son walk home arm in arm.

At an odd moment during the day, they recover the lost balls, now lying brightly exposed against the turf. In most cases, the number retrieved equals the number lost, unless an errant ball has rolled into the tall grass that borders the field. For every ball that is thrown into the air, a ball falls to the ground. Only the foibles of eyesight prevent a full accounting of each evening's throw. That is the premise of their evening game and their search the following day.

As the summer days shorten, the man and his son begin to lose more balls than ever before. The discrepancy first becomes apparent when the field and tall grass yield so few balls during the day. They wonder whether playful dogs or other animals are making off with the balls. The puzzle intensifies during early evening when the white balls are still quite visible. Thrower and catcher follow a thrown ball to its zenith. At that point, the ball fails to descend and somehow disappears.

Their game takes on a new dimension. They have an eerie feeling that a third player has joined them above. From time to time, he mischievously intercepts a ball in midair and refuses to throw it down. The man and his son now contend with both the third player and the darkening sky as they throw balls back and forth. They even abandon their daily search for missing balls, concluding that most, if not all, remain above. Soon the game becomes dissatisfying, as they lose the confidence that every ball thrown up will come down.

By the end of summer, the few remaining white balls rest unused in the bucket. The man and son turn to other games at twilight and rarely talk about the disappearing balls. They find the puzzle demeaning, depriving them of the pleasure of a game determined solely by human skill. To inject an alien factor denies that pleasure.

After several days of heavy rain, the two cross the field one evening, returning from a walk. They see several fairy rings of mushrooms that have grown up from the damp turf. The mushrooms are round and white, very much like the balls in the bucket. Indeed, to their astonishment, the mushrooms are the balls, finally descended from the sky. They eagerly gather up the balls and begin throwing them as high as they can into the darkening sky. They are totally absorbed in each ball's ascent and heedless of its descent—now or ever.

Arthur G. Dove, *Dark Abstraction,* **1921**

KEEP

Keep my own am I
And palisade,
Hoist to drawbridge quick
Against dire raid.

Lofty battlement
Behind I lurk,
Crenels through espy
Afar foe's work.

Moated enemy
I now abhor:
Ambient pool back hurls
Self whom I war.

PRESENCES

The old man had served as first mate on tramp steamers. During his voyages, he had experienced exotic places and encountered esoteric ideas. Now dwelling in a cottage by the estuary, he reflected upon all the good and evil the oceans had brought him. Enlivened by the infinite play of waves, he considered himself, with pride, a skeptic. His power of speculation was as acute as his propensity for doubt.

With a sailor's sense of tidiness, he kept his cottage in apple-pie order. Each piece of furniture and china had its proper place. Functionality yielded only to wild flowers he gathered and set about in vases. Their random sprays and colors intensified the vertical and horizontal lines that dominated the cottage. He often thought that blindness would hardly interfere with the use and enjoyment of his ordered realm.

The disturbances began in the cupboard. From time to time, he found the pieces of china in disarray. Saucers were transposed with the cups, and plates were stacked upside down. Bemused, he set them back in their proper place. Curiously, the disarray increased after he affixed slip-free latches to the cupboard doors. The latches seemed to provoke whatever presences were responsible.

The disturbances then got out of hand. Returning from his walks along the beach, he found furniture thrown about, sheets and blankets torn from the bed, and flowers strewn on the floor. In his remote cottage, he had never felt the need to secure it against strangers. He was now driven to shutter the windows and bolt the doors. The greater the precautions he took, however, the more mischievous the presences became. He spent much of his time restoring his cottage to order after their frequent deviltries.

Finally, contrary to his temperament, he decided to cease resisting the presences. The skeptic in him recognized that this assumed their existence. He justified the assumption on pragmatic grounds, suspending its metaphysical implications. Latches and bolts were removed, shutters taken down. He grudgingly accepted the disarray, and, as he did so, it began to diminish. If certain objects continued to be shifted out of place, he left them there. If the order of his favorite books was improper, so be it.

In time, the condition of his cottage returned to normalcy. He recognized, however, that he would never be normal again. Incomprehensibly but tellingly, he had accepted the presences and their constant activity about him. No longer did he dwell alone in his cottage by the estuary. However absurd to the skeptic, this fact was now beyond dispute and prompted rich, new speculations. He had made peace with the presences—and with himself.

ANNO DOMINI

That first morning, she rose early to the songbirds' ubiquity. To her surprise, she was moved to offer up the fragment of a prayer recalled from childhood. Leaving her lover sleeping, she quietly closed the door, pondering its inviting and forbidding mien.

Outdoors, in the wondrous air, she felt invested with new time. Like a soft, sun-dried shirt, it cherished her. Purged of the febrile past, she succumbed to its languor. Moments condensed into brilliant balls she juggled with grateful hands. She even spied bits of time flowing backwards—or was it forwards?—to creation.

She returned to the house to stand at her writing table. Composing the landscape before her eyes, she began to write a letter to herself. Her words spilled out like toy soldiers on the playroom rug. Their order was unimportant; they seemed to witness the presence of new time.

Finishing the letter, she remembered the cornerstone of the local church with its worn Roman numerals. She paused and then resolved to crown her letter. With a flourish, she wrote the date—"1 January, 1 A.D." Looking out upon creation, she devoutly hoped she could do the same tomorrow.

VISIONS

A brilliance swift
Incarnadine
Rends yet restores
My fragile self.

Declare then I:
A cardinal
Across the lawn
This morning flew.

My puny world
I thus compose
And blast again
Edenic sight.

ELDERS

City park's bright fountains by
Yellowed bench on elders sit
And fedoras black beneath
Gestured densely words emit.

Huddled sun against they face
Backwards   down   thronged   streets   of
boys,
Scrawling dust at feet with sticks,
Of forgotten guardians' toys.

Troops of booted war and peace
Through unknowing eyes and naps
Agelessly have they observed,
Humming martial tunes of scraps.

HOPSCOTCH

On the city sidewalk, the children avidly played hopscotch. From its transverse divisions, they hung adjoining rect-angles with red and yellow chalk. Within the prescribed grid, the children cast and returned the prize, hopping back and forth on one foot and then two. After due deliberation, the city fathers proscribed hopscotch on the city sidewalk, proclaiming it to be an impediment to pedestrian traffic. To their consternation, the divisions on the sidewalk be-gan to expand, creating dangerous fissures. The separation between the sections grew from inches to feet, and pedes-trians were in danger of falling irretrievably into the abyss. The street soon became a series of depthless canyons, too deep even to sustain an echo. In desperation, the city fathers reinstated hopscotch. The sections of the sidewalk began to come together again, and the children joyfully resumed their game—with each hop healing a break.

Arthur G. Dove, *Sun Drawing Water*, 1933

8

Peak Experiences

As I scan the landscape of my life, here and there I see brilliant pulsations of light. These pulsations combine, in varying degrees of intensity, the luminous and the numinous. That is, they give off a perceptible light, and simultaneously intimate the Divine. I am sketching below five instances of these pulsations, which may be called peak experiences.

FIRST PEAK EXPERIENCE

When I was about thirteen, I spent several weeks with a friend at his summer house in Ogunquit, Maine. Having arrived the prior evening, I was anxious to rise early and explore the house and its environment. Before the household awoke, I tiptoed downstairs and walked onto the balcony. I stood there surveying my demesne—the inlet, beach, surf, and Atlantic Ocean below me.

I confronted the miracle of a fresh new day, capping the millions of prior days. The brilliant and powerful sunlight emerged from the flawlessly blue sky. It struck the water with the intensity of a lion's roar. The golden cannonade then ricocheted off the surface of the waves to the limitless sky above. It seemed that these events never ceased but kept repeating themselves for as long as I stayed on the balcony. After all these years, I can still draw upon the profound freshness of the events.

SECOND PEAK EXPERIENCE

In 1967, I served as a government lawyer engaged in negotiating trade agreements with other countries. In this capacity, I made frequent trips to Geneva, Switzerland, where the negotiations were taking place. On one occasion, I rented a modest room in the old city.

The room was dark and cold, without heat. A black and heavy rain fell outside the French windows, and gargled mournfully in the gutters. I heaped my bed with blankets to create a warm cocoon against the ambient chill. I burrowed deeply into my cave, alone and content. The cave descended into the earth. Far from feeling immured, I experienced a sense of release far from diurnal cares. After what seemed to be several hours, with sadness I emerged from my caring cave. To this day, I frequently invoke this image as I fall asleep. It is hugely reassuring.

CALL

The young man was far from home, in a strange city. During his few days there, he spent most of the time languishing in his hotel room. He awoke late, had his meals brought to the room, and read voraciously. His occasional excursions in the hotel's district sharpened his pleasure at the insularity of his room. From time to time, he made and received telephone calls to and from friends at home. These calls both annoyed and pleased him, serving to juxtapose their distant community and his immediate solitude. But from one young woman he hoped especially to hear, and he evoked in his mind her shy speech and ill-suppressed warmth. As he packed his bag to leave on the last day of his stay, he heard her voice again with rare clarity. He left the room, delighted and grateful that she had never placed the call.

THIRD PEAK EXPERIENCE

In 1951, when I was a junior at college, I took a course on Proust, Mann, and Joyce. It was given by a renowned professor of comparative literature. Among the required readings was Mann's novella, *Death in Venice*. On a Saturday morning, I went to the library and took the work down from its shelf. My chair was comfortable, the light good. The inside distractions were few, and the outside noise was muffled. I was ready to embark on a literary voyage that would last several hours.

The novella begins in Munich and ends in Venice before World War I. It concerns a German novelist, Aschenbach, who falls in love with a beautiful adolescent boy, Tadzio, while visiting Venice.

From the opening, the novella had me in its grip to an unexpected degree. Normally a rapid reader, my pace in this case was deliberate and even slow. I wanted to relish the story and its characters, to be sure. But I also needed to savor each paragraph, each sentence, even each word. They were like succulent foods, to be slowly and fully tasted on the palate.

As I continued reading, I became convinced that every word was perfectly and inescapably chosen. The words formed an elaborate mosaic, in which each stone took its predestined place. The text of the novella flowed without flaw, and I was enraptured. I knew then that I had been privy to an aesthetic experience of a rare order.

THREE QUARTETS

A green freshman, I was still getting my bearings in my undergraduate college. One of my friends suggested that we attend a recital that was being offered on campus free of charge. I agreed without the slightest idea of what I was getting into.

According to the program, the recital featured the Budapest String Quartet playing three quartets commissioned by Count Razumovsky and composed by Ludwig van Beethoven. I knew some of Beethoven's works, but none of his chamber music. The two violinists, violist, and violon-cellist came onto the stage in stark black dinner jackets. They seemed intense and austere, as though practicing an arcane art.

From the first to last bars, I was enthralled and stupefied. The composer and the players held me in their grip. I was carried away by the shifting sonorities and undergirding rhythms. But I had neither the intellectual nor emotional comprehension of what I was hearing. Yet the successive movements of all thee quartets were making demands upon my psyche, leading me into a realm I had never been before.

At the conclusion of the recital, the audience burst into loud applause. But I wished that the audience had thanked the four players with total silence. I wanted to hold onto the remains of the recital as long as I could.

I have since heard the Razumovsky Quartets a number of times. After two hundred years, they continue to celebrate the human spirit in wondrous ways.

JOURNEY

The old man awoke with the clear and expectant conviction that he would die that afternoon. He had long put his affairs in order, including the execution of a modest will and firm instructions concerning his cremation. Now he had only a few spiritual obligations to fulfill. He set out extra food for his cats, in case his neighbors failed to look in for a few days. He put fresh water in the several vases of luminous fall flowers. And for the last time he wound the grandfather clock he remembered as a boy. After lunch and a stroll along the quickly flowing river, he lay down for his daily nap. In spite of the biting arthritis in his legs, he was pleasantly tired and happy to give himself over to sleep. He awoke after sundown, chagrined that he had overslept. Or had he already begun the next stage of his onward journey?

FOURTH PEAK EXPERIENCE

In the summer of 1980, I spent several weeks in Dortmund, Germany, assisting a company involved in a lawsuit. One Saturday morning, a friend took me to an outdoor museum of medieval machines. Spread out over several acres, they were as much as five hundred years old. Though weathered, they seemed to be in sound and even working condition.

I was first struck by the aesthetic quality of the machines. They revealed a sensitivity to shape, balance, and materials. Some of the machines bore a striking resemblance to twentieth-century sculpture. Visitors were encouraged to run their hands over the machines.

As I continued to stroll among the machines, I suddenly grasped their underlying principle. I saw the machines as fundamental congeries of assembled parts, set in motion by energy. The parts represented the fission of a fragment of reality. Indeed, they constituted nothing less than an attack upon reality. Thus was laid the foundation of the fateful opposition of analysis and synthesis.

TIGER SWALLOWTAILS

The elderly man stood at the busy downtown intersection. He held an open umbrella against the sun shower. Gusts of wind tossed sheets of newspapers about and made their colored pages soar. As he watched, a cluster of butterflies emerged from the variegated pages. He recognized them as tiger swallowtails from his butterfly-collecting days. The cluster bobbed erratically on the wind. They flew so low at times he feared they might be crushed between the sharp umbrellas. To his surprise, the pedestrians took no note of their brilliant flight. As the sun shower stopped, the wind abated. The now-sodden pages fluttered down and came to rest against the curb. The tiger swallowtails had vanished.

FIFTH PEAK EXPERIENCE

In the fall of 1975, my wife served as a member of the vestry of our Episcopal church. At the time, I was not a Christian but rather an unhappy agnostic. But I agreed to accompany her to a vestry retreat at a Roman Catholic cloister called Manresa.

At the close of the retreat, we all held hands to form a circle in celebration of the Holy Communion. The person to my right passed me a basket filled with chunks of homemade bread, saying "The body of Christ, the bread of heaven." The same person passed me a cup containing watered port, saying "The blood of Christ, the cup of salvation." I was expected to eat of the bread and drink of the wine and repeat the same litany to the person to my left. But I could not, reduced to mumbling something inane about the love of God.

These all-too-conspicuous lapses were the source of my deep anger and intense longing. It would take some years to overcome these hurdles to a sound relationship.

Arthur G. Dove (1880-1946) © *Willows*, 1940
Oil on gesso on canvas, 25 x 35" (63.5 x 88.9 cm)
Gift of Duncan Phillips
Location: The Museum of Modern Art, New York, NY, U.S.A.
Photo Credit: Digital Image © The Museum of Modern Art/Licensed
by SCALA / Art Resource, N.Y.
© The Estate of Arthur G. Dove, courtesy of Terry Dintenfass, Inc.

IMAGES

The first image falls within the bounds of time and space.

In the late 1930s, Arthur Dove, the now-renowned American painter and his wife, Reds, my mother's sister, lived in a one-room house that was previously a post office located on an inlet in Centerpoint, Long Island. It reflected a tidy and pervasive poverty. Furnishings were minimal, and frugal clothes smelled of the sea.

Most Sunday afternoons my father, mother and I would drive to the little house to spend a few hours with Reds and Arthur. As I ran in and out of the house, I caught snippets of what struck me as a tedious and desultory conversation. But at a certain point, the tenor of the conversation became at once leaner and warmer, and I knew that Arthur was sharing his newest paintings, both finished and unfinished. He was met by expressions of delight and encouragement, both of which I sensed he badly needed.

The second image is the product of my imagination. It captures Arthur alone in the little house. The furnishings recede into insubstantiality. Sadness lurks in the corners.

Arthur is seated before the easel and looks intently out the window. Before him loom sea, sky, and earth—his raw materials. They inform his cosmos, which is given to infinite permutations of line and color.

Like the true artist, he wields his brush in a self-absorbed trance. The shapes of nature undergo a metamorphosis, so that the seen reveals the unseen. Beneath the brush the real and surreal merge. The distinction between the observed and the created dissolves.

Over the years, this image of the fiercely dedicated artist has intensified in my mind. Silhouetted against the window, his stature has steadily grown.

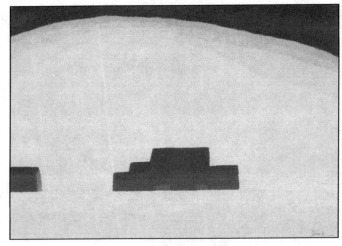

Arthur G. Dove, *Snow Thaw,* **1930**

9

Epilogue

FISH

During the temperate months, my father, mother, and I lived in a primitive farmhouse outside of Paris. With the house came a menagerie consisting of one goat, two rabbits, three doves, and a cat. They were the members of a rudimentary circus that I staged from time to time.

Next door lived Michel, my best friend. We were inseparable, sharing the experiences of a rural setting. I spent many hours with Michel in his mother's warm and redolent kitchen. I can recall, in particular, her legerdemain in paring a pumpkin into a single orange ribbon.

Occasionally, I accompanied Michel to the local church, where he and his family worshipped someone called Jesus Christ. I knew nothing about this man, but I suspected that he gave off a special aura. I stayed outside the church, overhearing fragments of an unintelligible language. At the end of the service, Michel rejoined me.

There came a day that Michel's mother called Easter Sunday. She explained that, in his honor, Michel and I were to search for an Easter surprise in her vegetable garden. We could not wait to start.

We began to search in a helter-skelter fashion. When this yielded nothing, we adopted a more methodical approach. The carrots, peas, and cabbages proved to conceal nothing, and I moved onto the lettuce.

I pulled back a particularly large leaf. To my astonishment, I exposed a large fish that appeared to be made of milk chocolate. It had a thick shell and a hollow inside. Michel and I ran to show the chocolate fish to his mother. She seemed delighted and broke two pieces off, one for Michel and one for me. I asked her what Jesus Christ had to do with the fish. She replied enigmatically that they were one and the same. I went on munching the fish.

Note: Many years later, I learned that ixthus is not only the Greek word for fish, but also the acronym for Jesus Christ, as follows:

I(esus)	Iesus
x(ristus)	Christus
th(eou)	of God
u(ios)	son [and]
s(oter)	savior

Hence, Jesus Christ, Son of God and savior (of humanity).

SHADOW

A summer afternoon:
The door shifts to a breeze.
I hear its shadow lurch,
The beating of moth's wings.

His silence is as loud:
Dead to the stopped-up ear,
And thunder to the quick.
Now catch the shadow grow.

GARDENER

Without looking back, she steps out of the hollow's shadow and begins to run. She must hurry to explain her astonishment to the others.

At the crest of the hill unexpectedly appears the gardener. He stands tall, enveloped by the morning run at his back. He bids her cool her feet in the pebbled stream. Annoyed yet curious, she sits down on the bank.

"Why are you hurrying so?" he asks.

"I must deliver a vital message," she replies.

"A matter of life and death?"

"Both, I think."

"Whose?" he poses.

"I am not certain. It may implicate us all."

"How do you propose to find out?"

His insistent questions seem a row of traps. She falls silent, letting her feet drift in the cool water. She must be on her way.

More gently, he wonders aloud, "At the edge of the garden, were you terrified by your emptiness—or mine?"

Straining to make sense of his question, she essays, "His emptiness made me believe that he is fulfilled elsewhere."

"So your terror began to turn to joy?"

"Creating a second terror that my joy might be unfounded."

"Fright," he rejoins, "is born of what we see, joy of what we seek."

Kneeling before her, he replaces the sandals on her feet. As she resumes her journey, he smiles and raises his right hand in farewell.

Going more slowly than before, she ponders her strange meeting with the gardener. In his presence, terror was succeeded by expectation, and expectation by incipient joy. Yet she sees no cause for joy about her.

She stops along the way. Closing her eyes, she again encounters the gardener in the morning sun. He beckons to her, and she races back to the garden. She is not disappointed to see him absent, since his presence is heartfelt. Her message is now as clear as the pebbles in the stream.

ANNIVERSARY

My self ripped out of self:
Abstraction Christ did work
Now many years ago
That I might touch the life.

My self reclaiming self:
The whole Christ will not shirk
In his monistic flow,
Lest hell renew its strife.

Arthur G. Dove, *Flour Mill II,* **1938**